We Call Them Beautiful

KC Trommer

First Edition 2019 ©KC Trommer
All rights reserved.
ISBN: 978-1-939728-29-6
Diode Editions
Doha, Qatar
Richmond, VA
Design & layout: Law Alsobrook
Cover art: KC Trommer
Author photo: Sylvie Rosokoff
Ordering & Contact information: http://www.diodeeditions.com

For my mother — and hers

The ability to tell your own story, in words or images, is already a victory, already a revolt.

— Rebecca Solnit, "Grandmother Spider"

What we see, we see
and seeing is changing.

— Adrienne Rich, "Planetarium"

First Map

Stone fences lined the road to the art academy
where the teacher unscrolled the butcher paper

                    on the floor, told me to lie down. I fanned my fingers
                and spread my legs as a boy drew my outline in marker.

The ceiling was so far up, the cement floor cold against my back
and the smell of the room was the smell

                      of drying acrylic. I stood up from the paper
                and my body was an outline inside the sneaker prints

of the boy who had drawn me. The teacher handed me a pen,
said, *Now, fill in the rest.*

I

Jaws (1975)

Before *Jaws*, I only cared about the jellyfish that ballooned
on the waves in loose clusters, humming with danger. I didn't close my eyes then,
never. I did the flips and watched everything upside
down and dizzy whirl over my bent knees. Even now, swimming with him,
I stay close to the shore. I wade up to my chest and stop.

I feel everything swim between my legs: the water cooler here,
warmer there. Is it better to tread water or to float? I turn my body up
like one of the jellyfish, collect the sun. He always wants to go farther, so I watch
as his arms move in furious little triangles toward Europe.

When I tread water, I picture how the shark would see me:
the legs waving *hello*, pulled into the dark theater, where the man's head floats
across the screen as fear shoots life into my nerves, up and down, and he swims back
to me, kisses my mouth and presses hard against me. There's salt
in our kiss. How do we look from below?

Surface Anatomy of the Head and Neck

My mother brushes her hair in bed, the hard brush
against her scalp. No pliable bristles, just plastic teeth
that dig in. I would rather an easier, less punishing instrument.

At night, I need to soften the place where my neck meets
my shoulders. I rub out the debris of who was late and how
late they were, of the word I meant to learn the full meaning of
but used anyway, of the woman I meant to molt but instead keep wearing.

When he drives, I grip the back of his neck, hold my fingers stiff
like claws, move them over the surface. Plates of the head like plates
in the earth and the pressure and relief, necessary. He closes his eyes

for a moment but the car keeps going. The mother cat grabs her
mewlings by the scruffs to carry them to the darkest corner of the barn.
I pick them up in the same place as if to say, *Listen, I'm your mother now.*

Mica

winks from the rocks on the pond as I climb from
the water like an early fish, on short, new legs.
 The rock face sheds a layer of mica scales that drift
into my hands. From the Latin *micare* — to shine.
 It's like having a permanent sunburn, he once said. Always
ashamed, hiding his scales under long pants even
 on hot days. When we sat on the rocks, I touched
his leg gently as if being gentle would soothe. *It itches like hell*.
 He took his knife, to make a show of it — the sharp edge scraping
away plaques of skin — sighed, littered himself on the ground.
 Some days, he could not walk because his feet bled. The *vulgaris*
in *psoriasis vulgaris* means common. Split yellow fingernails,
 his hand wrapping my shoulder. Smell of tar shampoo, smell
of Bay Rum and Swisher Sweet cigars. Stale coffee.
 The smells are with me, drifting into me as I walk through the city.
He was on the rock when I slipped back in the pond.
 From the water, I called, *Come in, Dad, come in*.

Meat Cove, Cape Breton

Up
at
four,
out
to
load
the
traps
onto
the
boat.
What we pulled up we did not always save. The hair of
my arms bristled in the cold. In an earlier evolution, this
would have made me seem larger, less vulnerable to
attack. The traps came up clicking, lobsters brown and
mottled with little eyes that had no whites to roll in, just
wet nubs that came up out of their armor, under their
horns. I held the pinching claws away from me, measured
from the rear of the eye socket along the center body shell.
I checked under the tails for eggs, dropped the mothers
back in. They fell through the water to settle softly on the
bottom. This is how we trained them to trust the traps.

The Hasp Tongue

The sucker mouths of the lampreys open
to show a circle of vampire teeth. Their bodies wave out
behind them. They were once eaten by kings —
one died of a surfeit of lampreys.

When we swim, we swim with them.
You laugh at me and jump in, arms then
shoulders then the steaming mass of your head,
shed horseflies from your skull.

Another circle within the first mouth circle: *vagina dentata*.
Who can see them and not think it?
Mouth circle with rows of layered teeth where Virgil
walks, Dante trailing him, into the mouth,

down the next flight of teeth, along the hasp tongue
and into the blood-filled belly of the lamprey.
Fixed to the side of a bass, it will suck,
the mouth working everything out.

Some hatch, toothless, in fresh water,
mature in the ocean, come back to fresh water to feed.
I keep calling this ocean, but there's no salt.
We see our toes as we test Lake Superior.

Strange, nothing here. No seaweed bladders, no gulls picking
through driftwood. You swim to me and I see you
before you grab my legs. We weave inside and out
of the Painted Rocks, wave at the pontoon boats

before dipping our heads back underwater.
You keep your eyes open as you swim.
The water makes us loose confederates,
swimmers whose heads bob above the surface.

The Cyclone

I don't understand you the way I don't understand
roller coasters, why people lock themselves
into rickety rides to be reminded — repeatedly —
they are going to die   little deaths —

The personality book asked me what
I felt when I imagined riding a rollercoaster. *Dread*, I thought.
The next page said the rollercoaster represents sex.

I felt   the dip in my stomach
                         I knew before I knew
roller coasters and wanted to tell the book about my roaring
          twenties,   how I went bravely over the clattering tracks, locked in,   white
knuckled   screaming   rounding the same corners   to feel   I was alive
                         and sex mine to ride

how much of our bodies are water — the nerves, a net of Christmas lights thrown over us

On Coney Island, the screams of the Cyclone riders
whip around like streamers — I want to point them out to you, ask if you recognize them
               or if there is a girl up there,
                              in a striped shirt, tilting back, eyes closed,   laughing her head off —

Scylla, Dragging at the Hounds

On the shelves around us, the books are closed.
I read the story of Scylla, how she was split
and split again, dragging at the hounds she fled from.
When he shows, I notice his beard is going gray and he drags
out the same old, same old story. His want never slows. It's the same
for Scylla as it is for me: the corrosive of love marked me
his. That I did not want to be claimed does not matter —
half of him drags at me even as I shut him up inside,
seem woman to the waist and fair.

We Call Them Beautiful

We have decided to love trees. The living ones
        are corralled along the sidewalks in cities.
           The dying ones, once glorious,
                    collapsed into dust from not being seen.
           Those in forests
                wave their hair and hands whenever the wind blows.

When he runs the track, they are behind him and all around the park.

           Against the grey sky, they are like nerves pulled from the body,
      waving, sucking air, sucking dirt.

He starts clean but comes around
               the seventh time sweating, soaking his shirt through,
                giving me a little wave for my whistle.

A sliver of Einstein's brain blown up under the microscope shows
               all the branches
          of where his thoughts went. Still waving.

      Around the track the trees wave through the grey afternoon sky,
            like mute women trying to alert me to an emergency.

Gauntlet

You thought you were brave before. No.
You must be braver.

All their thick mitts are mad to strike
you. You must be braver.

Follow the course to the end
of the course. Of course, all their pinprick eyes love

to stick you. Be braver. The race is not yet done,
not by half, and every savage tongue

lives to whip you. Braver. This, all this,
is the making of you.

You thought you were brave
before. No. No, you must be braver.

II

Bench (1999)

All the scenes I remember of us are interiors, except the summer day we went to the Noguchi. Before the archway to the sculpture garden, I started to sit down on a bench and you gathered my right arm gently in your hand, pulling me up and saying *ah-ah-ah* while pointing at the sign that said PLEASE DO NOT TOUCH. Next to it, the museum label read: *Bench* (1966). I laughed and you said, *That is the difference between you and me, right there.*

Oh, but Noguchi would have wanted me to sit on *Bench* and — for that matter — to touch every one of his sculptures, those smoothed stones and soft polished wood that seem to call for hands.

You were right, of course. If it looks like a bench and I am tired after walking, I will sit. I will not be careful; I will not read the fine print. I will take it at its word. I will trust that it will hold me for as long as I need to be held.

7 to 46th Street/Bliss

When the train picks up speed, it sounds like a woman screaming,
one woman all over the city, releasing her heat in a high, steady wail,

smearing her red mouth along the tunnel walls. I make and unmake
myself. When the doors open, anyone can come in, anyone does. I circle back

downtown, leave the book open on my lap, look over the map
that lays out the routes. The city is a muscle; we feed it. The woman across

from me shrivels up her face, sticks a finger in each ear to kill the sound
of the train rounding into Queensboro Plaza. My hands are warm

on my lap: they are for making and unmaking. I thumb the seam
of the sketchbook open while the city sits and waits, indifferent and unblinking

like all gods. My mouth is a siren, my body mine to make.
Wherever I go, I am this woman. Whoever needs erasing, I erase.

Written Under the Arch

Whirring behind clock time, the steady bliss
of perfect time now clicks out its dry song.
Some physicists will tell you that time is
what clocks measure, even when clocks are wrong.
Perhaps Janus knows the secret, stone still,
facing forward and looking back, guarding
neither what has come to us nor what will,
our witness that time is here, now bending,
now breaking. Tell us, Janus, what the clocks
and physicists deny: that time is more
than mechanism, it burns open the locks
to deliver us to the waiting store
of memories new-made and memories shuttered.
Each word we utter a word we've uttered.

The Flageolet Player on the Cliff

is the least of it, blowing soft notes
from the painting's far corner, along

a thread of road
as the maid faces us, her back to

a cliff that keeps dropping
into the ocean.

Your thigh is warm against
mine. I can't stop looking

and everything is alive
and moving.

I want to go back and line up next to you,
to lift the pain from behind your eyes and feed it

to the painting which understands how everything
turns and is turning and never keeps you safe.

Down the hall, the angels stand stark behind you.
You cower, even though their wings are still.

Why not be the one who pours open the sky,
and lets cliffs do as the ocean does?

You let slip a grimace.
Let me smooth it away,

like notes from the song he plays from the green edge
where we sit still, and I am always turning to you —

After Looking at Bontecou's *Untitled* (1961)

I impress them with my appetites, scare them with how much want there is,
                                                             there always is —

Want darker than my childhood upturned over dinner, spilled out and running black
along the base of our water glasses, over the edges of the linen
to pool around our ankles

It's blacker than a night in the woods after a year of city living, black against
the sound of car tires
          streaming past the bed you should be sleeping in.
                                        Black as that and nothing will light it up.

It will not be appeased.
You cannot leaven it.
It takes the light back from your lamp as soon as you snap it on.

Pit black like a Bontecou maw and calling out   from space,
                                        from the underside of the angler fish
                                        from every opening   opening

This want started small,
          a period pressed in ink to the end of the line.
                                        A finish that started it.

          Why not show it all upfront, over dinner, over drinks, over my dead body,
          living here
                    in the pulse of want. Wanting here
                    to envelop, surrender, smile into it, open wide
                              my mouth until the mouth demonstrates finally the scope of it,
                              takes want into my innards creaking solemnly inside
                                        like a warship crawling through the Pacific,
                                        eluding radar, barreling along and full of men,
                                        ready to strike.

Magritte's *The Titanic Days* (1928)

Someone is playing a trick on me.
I see the approach. Her body is the frame.
When I fall back to sleep, another nightmare waits.

He is the one I wrest against, and his the only name.
Her body is the frame he enters; her body is mine.
I know when someone is playing a trick on me.

He wears a suit. She is naked; the struggle in her face is plain.
I know how she tries and fails to rewind.
I fall asleep again, and another nightmare waits.

Why didn't he call it *le viol*? Clothed and naked, I feel her shame.
He hasn't won: she's just not free while they're intertwined.
He hasn't won: I know someone is playing a trick on me.

The catch is to guard against him and never be tamed.
But such words are nothing when you hear her whine.
When I fall asleep again, a nightmare waits.

We see the back of his head and her body is the frame.
The struggle is in her — her arms force away his vines.
Someone is playing a trick on me.
When I fall asleep, another nightmare waits.

Off the Roosie

After O'Hara

I get off the 7 and head home, past the Chase and the Jackson Heights
      penguin that, last week, someone dressed as a bunny, and I'm thinking
of Frankie's I-do-this-I-do-that poems, and my phone is dead again
      and I can't afford to replace it. All I want to hear is Spoon
singing *got no regard for the things you don't understand*
      but maybe, as Lorna said, it's a gift and there's a poem across the street
waving *Yoo hoo! Over here!* and trying very hard to get
      my attention. I get onto 37th, near what's left of the Brunson Building
after the fire on Easter Monday and I head past the Met (not that one)
      which they renamed Foodtown but which Honor and Joe and I
will always call the Met (not that one), and then a left onto 77th
      and past our coffee shop where Afsal stands outside, talking,
but for once does not say hello even though he looks
      straight at me, and it's fine, I walk past the Berkeley and over 35th Ave.,
and I guess I'm home, considering that my keys have opened
      the door even before I realized I had them in my hand, and everything
is where I left it, even in the bedroom where I keep waking alone quite
      suddenly to find — yes, I left you. You've never even been here.

The Light Table

She places the glass on top of the vellum, puts down
a stand of trees. Around her, textured, beveled, clotted,

I hear the arch ache of glass against glass.

The sheets lean against each other, under her.
Her knees are bracketed by a clear pane, a sheet of green.

One — for the birches — is cataract white.

Pressing through the base of her thumbs, she funnels
her full weight down into the tip of the glass cutter.

She stops, knocks a tree limb from the sheet.

She lays the puzzle of it piece by piece on the light table,
spreads Liquid Flux over the glass.

Copper tape glints around the edges.

With the soldering iron, she guides the silver solder over the edges, fusing
the birches in a net of light, each one bound to the one beside it.

Smoke drifts up and it looks as if her hair
is beginning to catch fire.

Diptych

Recto

Nailed to wall of the barn,
    it leaks oil. A Renaissance angel
    hovers inside the blue and red.

You give it to me, call it First of the Last.
    I sit close and wait
    for the next one to appear.

My arms don't want to lift me up
    out of the chair. When can I thank you?
    No time is right.

Verso

Too naked in my suit to be with you, alone.

We walk out to where the river
    deepens, twelve feet of cool
    water straight to the bottom.
        So you say.

I want to trust you. I hold my breath
    and go down, feel the cool
    water slide me open.
        Where I touch bottom,
        the rocks barely shift.

Virtue

After The Ladder of Divine Ascent, Mt. Sinai

My skeleton is steady and my body moves
against the black. When the devils fall, I hear them falling —

At first, the only sounds are my hands
releasing and grasping, my feet hushing against the rungs

my hands have passed over. I think I am going up. The ladders tilt away
from me and where one ends, I take up another. Wings of the devils flap.

Cloak of my skin taut to muscle, muscle
a cloak for bone, bone a cloak for — ?

If the ladders do not go up, I am lost. Have I stuffed my soul
into the marrow? I hear the *shoosh, shoosh* when they fall —

If they fall, have their wings failed them? Maybe they are falling up,
flying, maybe I climb across but never up, maybe I am

a devil who knows only her body, who listens only
to her body moving through space, never pausing, rushing through

this black field of air. Hand on a rung, another. Beneath that sound is
something softer, the sound of calluses forming on my hands and feet.

III

Reformation

Go on worrying. See
that I want a new thing.

We slide into this sideways —
Let's another way: cautiously,

the mud sucking at our feet, air
swift against our cheeks,

reeds whispering in the marsh,
every sound amplified.

Church bells bother
spinsters and widowers.

Let's hear only this: the softening
mud of the wild mire into which

we step. The suck of it.
The pull.

Est! Est!! Est!!! Near the Bridge of Fists

The stray dog on the Ponte dei Pugni skitters sideways,
away from a tourist whose yellow umbrella
encircles her. We're off the grid that held us, locked in steady
worship of magnetic north, believing in the points of our cross.

Venice for the honeymoon, cliché that made some cut their eyes
at us and smile flinty smiles. Let them squint it out.
It's been like this for months now: wheat/chaff, wheat/chaff/chaff.
Who sees us? Who sees only himself?

We were married under a convex mirror and we see its like in a window
on the Calle di Mezzo Via, where a flower seller shoves a rose between
us. Like good New Yorkers, we refuse it. Wine is cheaper than water
in Punto!, the supermercato, urging us, *Go ahead* —

and we relent, and buy up bottles of Est! Est!! Est!!! We laugh and let
the throat-sound of the wine glug down into the open mouths of our glasses.

To love, that I could conjugate, but never "to be loved."
Always unspooling the thread, never feeling it catch. Now I see:
It's turning your full attention to the person who is turned to you.
The glass you hold up to him is not a mirror. It's a window.

A Tuesday Spot

After Graham

When the police beat them, the women did what she says women from her tribe would do to say *I am your mother. You are beating your mother:* they pulled the fabric from their breasts and shook them. The reporter does not understand, says so. The woman says, *Women are not strong like men. Their strength is not in their arms.*

Men are stronger than women, my father said once. *Define strength*, I said. *Physical strength*, he said. *No*, I said, and went out the front door, dug around the base of the house, and lifted it over my head to shake him out and out he fell like change.

This is where I rest my hands — where I want to be touched — flat palms against the breastbone. Here is where the soul lives. You do not believe in a soul.

We're looking for parking, you telling me *no such thing as a soul* and me pointing to what I think is a spot, there, but no, it's a hydrant. You say, *We're just energy.*

We circle the block and I tell you how women in India now have a law to protect them from being beaten by the men they live with. The women may now make their appeals to a judge, and now men must prove that they did not beat their wives, or daughters, or mothers-in-law.

I put my hands here, like this, over the open space that floods.

I wish I'd saved the photographs, my mother told me. *To show you.*

Why do I cover this place — because it floods? First my hands, like this, on my open chest. Then a prayer, to make it stop.

Laws and prayers are only words. We drive around again. You say, *What matters is what we do now*, and as you say it, a space opens up in front of us.

Another Brightness

She could always imagine the child,
and now it hovers inside, betrays its surprise.
Since June, her body has shown outside
what she wanted to contain. Her body is a window
closed first by fear, then boredom, now suddenly opening —
It has her, all right. She marshals toward the day.

Better to be a different sort of woman, she thinks. One day
she might get there, embrace it all, resist nothing, hold the child.
But for now, it's too sudden. They see it as an opening:
now the fix is in, now she will stop with the surprises.
They cannot wait to tamp her down, even as she opens the windows
that could ghost her away, even though there is an outside

they want her to forget. The apartment collapses outside
in, the plates and cups leaning away from the light of day.
Give that girl something to hold on to as she leans out the window
to see the tops of trees, all the while feeling the child
coming. Her husband says nothing's a surprise;
this was what they wanted. For him, it's an opening,

but for her, it's a door she can never shut. She marvels at the opening,
what it lets out. She wants what she thinks is outside
her, to trust herself and welcome the surprise —
But her head drags through the day,
and she cannot lift it, though she wants to say, *Here, child.*
to reassure it, herself. The blinds come down over the windows.

Alone, the city alights over the trees, windows
framing the solitude where once for her opening
seemed the only way. Now she folds her arms, thinks of the child
that will fill them, tries to remember when outside
was as full as what she found in her day.
She bequeaths this love to the boy — a boy! — the surprise

of it. What does she know about boys? Surprise!
She dares him to wonder at how each window
frames another brightness, how each day contains
boxes within boxes, each opening
to reveal a new delight. She stands outside
him, now a protector and not a child,
the surprises ever opening
windows to the world outside
into which every day, child, you must go.

Everything Falls Through Me

Now I know what she can do and I
marvel at her. There is no *it* now.
I marvel. It is not it. She is.

She used to pull along behind me
but now I hold her up. I soften
to her softness. I harden to protect her.

Once she was the vessel, collecting and pooling
whatever I threw into her.

Now she holds nothing.

The world touches her sides as it passes through;
The world is made brighter by the passage through.

Up

So often I think of everything I cannot tell you,
everything that will not translate across time.

If there is a camera, let it catch us, so you may see something
of this story that you are in when you are outside of it.

Let whatever it catches show you how you were loved,
a still of you, pulled up onto my lap, laughing.

In raising you, I track back. Over my shoulder, I see
the whole country behind me as I beat out a new path.

My mother tells me about after they'd all been taken away,
how her mother came to the schoolyard fence,

and Aunt Jan stopped short, said,
Better not. There'll be trouble.

My grandmother, looking at the backs of her girls
receding, her heart walking out of her chest.

And now, all the time, mine's broken
and mended, broken and mended,

I do not understand. But know this:
everything that I want for you is for you alone.

Bring me back with a kiss, my sweet boy.
There is this love. No other.

What stunned me was to learn that to love you
I had to ask for better, then to make it,

then better what I had bettered.
This doesn't stop.

I pull you up because you ask me *Up*,
and up up up I will pull you.

Fear Not, Mary

We were talking about the Annunciation
in her office — the moment when Mary looks up

from her reading to find Gabriel and the whole story
alive in front of her — when we heard them down the street,

bleating through megaphones about the Shirtwaist girls trapped
in the Asch Building who called out, who jumped,

who burned. This was after eight died in Midwood,
days before the office filled with the smoke

from 2nd and 7th, just after we heard about the black box,
and the deliberate sounds of the co-pilot clicking 150 people down

to death, the morning after I woke at 5, to the smell of gas
in the kitchen, snapped the knob to OFF, turned on

the fan and opened wide all the windows. I found him still,
asleep, his small breath going along as if there were

no emergency, as if he could keep going, as if fires never
ate whole buildings, as if danger were not always

pushing up against you, as if you could not be trapped, like those girls
on Washington and Greene, like those children in Midwood,

like the newlyweds on Germanwings Flight 9525,
like Mary in the story, as if we are not always at the mercy

of something, his breaths keep going,
the breathing soft, steady, and on.

Returns

Here are the pet names you will never call me again Here are the jokes that died between us Here are the letters you sent me when we first met Here is the sound of my laughter, remember it Here is the sound of me on the phone giving directions Here are all the unplayed messages from me, listen Here are the gifts I bought for your family, keep them Here are the photographs you never took of me Here are the vows I wrote for us Here are the other children I will never have with you Here is how my body looked Here is the memory of the day he was born Here are the things you praised me for Here is the strength I had then Here is the terror when you took him Here is your face screaming in mine Here is your back, turned Here is a month of silence Here is the park where you wanted to leave me Here are all the times I said *My husband* Here are the dead anniversaries Here is a letter from my lawyer, please read Here is me, not bankrupt yet, keep trying Here is my rage Here is me, destroyed but not destroyed Here are the papers for you to sign Here is my rage Here is a friend from high school and her husband, take them Here is a catalog of years, unspent Here is the evidence of how I loved you Here are the pictures from the wedding Here are the times I asked for what I needed Here is a list of what I left in the apartment Here is the way my body was in the dark Here are the stories I trusted you with Here is what my lawyer told me to tell you Here is my rage Here is what I wanted for us Here is a catalog of our failures Here is what I tell our son Here is when he needs to practice Here is what the teacher said about him Here is what he said about the boy he thought was his friend Here is his temperature Here are his medicines Here is the helmet Here is what I tell him Here is where is mother lives She is all you know of me now   Keep the rest

R to 74/Broadway

In the year that everything came apart
that would never go back together,

I would wait by the officers until
he brought him down the steps and to me,

as I stood next to another woman,
there for the same reason.

He descended the staircase,
holding my boy aloft. My boy

would see me
and sometimes turn away.

Once his father was gone,
he would climb me and kiss me, not let me

put him down. All the while, the officers
were watching, even though they tried to look

as if they did not see us, as if
they had not seen it all before.

Odes to Lost In-Laws

I.

You called yourself invisible when you hunkered down
with me in the corner, outside the clan's huddle.
When the holidays come, you must hate me for getting out,
leaving you a lonely satellite. One day you'll find yourself,
like me, cast out, looking up to trace the small orbit
that no longer holds gravity for either of us.

II.

A certain kind of girl, who grows up pressing
her face against the windows of other families,

might be forgiven for thinking marriage
could win her not only a husband but also a family —

It's what they say in wedding toasts, isn't it? —
It wasn't said at mine. This family I would never enter

let me sit nearby for a spell. What wishful thinking
to believe that understanding could be a kind

of ownership and that something that seemed to be a whole
might, if there was love in it, accommodate me.

III.

God, I wanted to meet her;
she was responsible for you.

I fell plop in love with you, hard
as a suspended piano falls
from six stories up —
the same way you dropped me —

If I think of it, I can feel it still:
my second fall
crashing around my first,
the same urgency pulling
me fast to earth.

IV.

You'd be in the barn, smoking, painting, welding, waiting,
wanting company, NPR on the radio, inch-thick oils hanging to
dry, in the studio that felt like a home for me — and you,
who would talk with me for hours about art, my brother.

Divorce swallows up everyone who gets near it, and it
took you in its gullet and spat you out on the other side of the country,
unknowable, unrecognizable, a sudden stranger.
It's wrong to say it was the divorce. It was you.

But divorce has its own its own gravity.
What it touches is always changed.

V.

And you.

You were no sisters to me.

Final Harvest

Once, there was nothing I would not say to you. Now, I lean
away from the words, the only things I have to let fly.
I am careful. I think: please, leave well
enough alone. Why tell you in this present tense
that I never conjugated the verb? Why say that, for me, nothing
will make love past now that it's been dredged up, uncorked?

I have other things to attend to: genies to cork,
food for the week to cook, a boy to get to bed, a life to lean
into in which you appear, then vanish. Nothing
solves this. Should I — what? — fly
your way, say it all? It would be tense;
it would yield nothing. I want put you well

enough away from me. I'll have to drown it again, a well
the only answer. I can get it back in the bottle, if I trust the cork
to contain it. Now is a matter of thinking of what tense
I choose to know you in. Are you the past that happens to lean
into the present? Are you here now, racing to me, a fly
that lands and alights, and comes, finally, to make no sense, nothing

following a pattern? I can force this back into the bottle, into nothing.
As easy as it was to remember how I love you, what grace to be well
rid of you again. Habit makes things possible. There is the world you fly
through, not slowing to see whom you touch. Then you cork
it, learn what was done can be done again. One only has lean
memories of who mattered and why. One only sees the tense

tighten around the word to constrict it, to circumscribe it. Tense
is only a matter of thinking: I loved you. That's all. It's nothing
anymore. Back in the bottle with you, wicked genie. I lean
toward myself, toward self-preservation. I can learn this well and
finally. I can make a habit of this. I can take the cork
and stop it. Here is the bottle, just a container. Here, it flies

from my hands. Here, a well for safekeeping, it flies
to the bottom and falls below the echo of the splash. Tense,
the air comes up around it to leave me without a cork,
without a bottle, without a thought of what is lost, knowing nothing
is lost. Nothing. Knowing it is only a matter of thinking well enough
of myself to say, that which I cannot have I lean

away from. What does not yield is nothing,
who does not love me enough is nothing. Leave well
enough alone. Leave everything you might call lean

to those who don't want more, for whom lean
is enough, for whom there is no feast. Well,
for whom there is no feast, there is no love, there's nothing.

IV

Our Arrangement

Just sex. Just that. That silly lie, we lie.

We agree to contain nothing, and to move in silence,
your body sliding against mine after sex,

when the body, known,
must feel the body that knew it.

All night, some part of you was aligned to some
part of me, gently. Gently, as if in holding

each other we held our past lovers. Yours, a proxy
for the body I once held, the one I knew as well as my own.

This second holding is a parentheses
around nothing —

not an echo for an echo has to contain
the first sound.

The grief that such touching brings,
reminding you how sweet —

Here is sweet again with a new familiar.

I remind myself you are better at this
than I am. You've had more practice.

I wake to you, all night
never having left you alone.

The Mechanism of Pleasure

for AH

The brain is three pounds of soft mass. It's the consistency
of pudding, one doctor told me, which put me off
pudding afterwards. He gestured, motion of a finger
going through it, and even made the wet sound
for something — the knife? — sliding in. *Easy to make a mistake.*

They worked in the most primitive part of the brain,
the area that governs pleasure. And because
it was the brain, they kept me awake for surgery.
I didn't know — they hadn't told me — what would happen when
they took their scalpels in to pry away
the tumor nestled against the base of my skull.
When they were close, they leaned in, hovering, faces taut
in anticipation of the glorious moment and so it came:

a soft touch to the reptilian brain and delight sprung out,
shooting my body with ecstasies. I shook the table, silver metal
of their instruments tittering as my eyes rolled behind my lids in
glories. But after, I saw the strangeness in their eyes,
the flat black of them all having seen me.

Room Tone

I hid in the women's bathroom till the train
was about to leave. When I sat down on the spoiled leather,
I thought I was safe. Then, his hands pressed wet
against the glass outside. *You're a worm*, I thought,
and felt cruel. He kept pushing his fingers up against
the glass. No longer tight and hot with power,
he seemed to dissolve.

In the hotel room, I lay down on the white coverlet,
the creases in the fabric tightening under my weight.
My intestines whirled and spat inside me like loose
telephone lines. There was a two-way radio by the headboard
that he told me had been used to spy on foreigners. *Like us*, he said
and kissed me and I let him kiss me, feeling the current go dead,
static for the radio, pleasure runnelling off my sides.

Heel & Key

You step it & grind it
You grind it & step it hard
into the soft leather of your soft shoe.

Dancing by the river's edge
to coax a small smile from her tilted head —
You fool! laughing, *You fool!*

Oh, you'll do it twice for a right grin.
Boot straps & boot slaps.

No one knows you better'n me.
No one knows you better'n me.

This is how you walk it: let the trip guide you to the soft bottom of the river.
This is how you turn it: follow the slap of the leather over to the other shore.

Hush

He was careful with the window,
eased it up while holding the window fan steady —

He nestled it into the leaves — it whirred same as she slept: bare, alone, quiet

The window was a mouth, open —
                    — he would fit himself into it, then her.

Careful to keep the rope from squeaking   best go slow

When the light went on, he felt like he was in a school play —

What makes a girl scream like that? Like what crawled
down her throat when she was born came barking out

      Motherfucker   *Motherfucker*

        top syllable clapping against the bottom, clamping his heels —

The leaves picked up as he ran, leaves and   *Motherfucker*   *Motherfucker*
dogging him all the way down the hill, right up to the porch door
      till he heard Ma's weight creak on the landing, her voice:
                    Where you been?

Static Electricity

Hum and glow of the alarm clock, green blink of the smoke
detector signaling the battery pulse, slow thrum
of the computer. The grandfather clock tick-tocks each step
to my door. Shadowed slouchers hang back from the bed, and
hands come around edge of the mattress. I press
a pillow along my seam to where he was. Should be. Something take
the place of him — Yank the cord from the socket,
quell the steadiness the clock belies. I would rather say this is only
architecture. Here's my room. These are my things.
Make yourself at home. Open a window if you want to smoke.
Sparks come off the blanket, flick around my knees and hips.
Who is holding me? I ask the room while the room is still.

Your Underwear

Since we broke up, I found a pair of your underwear in my hamper. I washed them. It feels very strange to have them, but you didn't leave anything else and I'm not about to call you up to come and get them. I want to get rid of them but part of me thinks it's wrong to throw away such perfectly nice underwear. Since they're underwear, I can't even donate them. I put them on once — they're clean! — but when I did I felt like a crossdresser. They upset me, your underwear. I can't solve all of their problems. They keep showing up in the laundry. They're like somebody else's kid from down the block who has big, lonely eyes and who always turns up around suppertime.

Housesitting for Ludwig

If the light bulb burns out while you're here, there are three more under the sink. –L.

All the houses I've loved have been either in the woods or next to the ocean *and* in the woods. I've never lived in any of them. Meril once took me to visit a man named Iggie — short for Ignatius — Larousic in Cape Breton. *Iggie*, I said, and *Yes?* he replied, as if his name were not absurd. *Can you tell me where the bathroom is?*

His house overlooked Bay St. Lawrence and, to reach it, Meril and I drove down a dirt road through a stretch of pines. The floors in the house were painted yellow. I only mention it because when Ludwig asked me to housesit for him, I thought it might be like that.

When I arrived at the cabin, the door was unlocked. There was an axe in the corner and a pan on the woodstove. Oatmeal in a tin jar beside it. On the cot was a pillow — what luxury! — on which he had left a greasy ghost of his sleeping head. There was a note to me on the bed.

After he hiked up the mountain to see the place, Meril said, with a thoughtful pull on his feeble, newly sprouted beard, *Objects contain the possibility of all situations.* He had read the *Tractatus* in the original — *well, la di dah*, I said when he first told me, even though I was impressed. I do love a polyglot.

Behind the door there was a small triangle of dirt that had been swept into the corner. Just there, behind the broom, as if the broom was ashamed of it. *Whereof one cannot speak, thereof one must be silent*, said Meril. *Yes, quite*, I said to him as I swept the dirt outside where it belongs.

What the Body Knows

Skulls of small, prehistoric elephants had a single
hole in the front. From this, we made the Cyclops.

Humans used to eat elephants. We eat to live.
We find food wherever we can.

When you jolt the bed, that's when
I know you're asleep.

Against my back, the tusks slide in,
one on either side, to lift me up.

They grow in my hands. I crane my neck,
open my mouth, tear leaves from the trees.

When I telescope back to the bed, I put my mouth wet on
your sleeping mouth, feed you what I found.

Role Reversal

Meaning: I am the one to put
your hand on my thigh.

I am the one to say I want you —
(I'll try not to.)

I am the one who wants more than
I am wanted. I am

the one who is dreaming of you
when I am with myself.

You disappeared.

And this, this is what
that feels like.

Here I am,
on the other side.

v

Puncture

Apply pressure. A dog's bite. As in a puncture strip, used to deflate tires. Pin in a balloon. A pen, a nail, a splinter, broken glass, almost any sharp object will do. A puncture wound on either side of the area just above the knee where the dog grasped with its jaws. Allow it to breathe freely. There were puncture wounds on the body, as from a knife, a scissor. A small hole piercing the skin. Often, a pin. A large abrasion to the right cheek. Can you see fatty tissue? Muscle? Clean the wound. Protect it. Does the object remain in the wound? If the object remains in the wound, if the wound is in the head, chest, or abdomen, unless it is small — Injuries to the right hip and side and a puncture wound in the center of the back. The wound may not bleed excessively, may heal quickly on its own. You may need urgent care. Is there a loss of feeling? Is there numbness?

First, the Match

Taken from inside the tree,
I was sheared away from the rest
who, yes, were also broken into bits.

I was cut clean then, and made
to pay attention to geometry, and answer
the blade's straight lines

They fitted me with a neat, red head
and tapped a cap on that.

The box was there to receive me;
I aligned with the other captives
and saw no light until one was selected
who did not return.

Dead months of silence until again,
another, and then me —
dragged out along the pavement
and then up to light.

Evisceration

It's not nerves, but
       survival. Let's call
     the sea cucumber Prometheus since,
         clever as he is,
         he expels his guts
              whenever a predator nears,
            and grows them back again in short order,
                 always ready to offer himself up —
                    a pragmatist,
                    though one who knows only a single story.

The Odds of It

For HJS

I feel a sour, American want rising in me on the 7 train
as the car comes up for air after Hunters Point, so I start to play
that ridiculous little thought game that seems to settle all scores:
What would I do if I won the lottery?

After I send half of it away to Uncle Sam and finish buying
everyone houses who needs houses, after I donate
like a Koch but to the places that would undo their work —
because it's that much and fantasy doesn't care about reason —
and just as I bank the rest,
I think of H.,
who isn't anymore
but is all the time showing up inside me, called to mind
by someone's casual mention of a restaurant in Astoria
that he and I talked about going to which we will never
because he isn't anymore, this lovely, dark boy who became
a man worth knowing, one who carried
so much of my history,
this person I lost and found and lost again.

The fucking injustice of it, the finding and losing,
of his being gone, never goes away.

I'm about to step onto the platform at Court Square,
some part of me still thinking what if I had more
because I want to be able
to stay in this place that keeps turning into gold
around me, because I must stay here
and don't know how to manage it and it seems,
in that old American way,
that I am not enough and I don't have enough and never will,
that only money makes things possible and the sky is tilting away
from me into darkness and I think of H., who isn't
anymore, who is all the time
and I think, Don't be a fool. You've already won
the lottery: you're alive.

Some Women

My hands grow tired of pulling tissues
out of the box. No magic in it anymore.
The last one pulled to the surface,
married at the hem to the next. As with the waterworks.
I am forever making tea, peppermint tea.
She manufactures tears for a cuddle.
She is one of the ones I prop up. I curdle.
I find no more good milk in me.
My jokes are sawdust stuffing up
the gates of my teeth. Must sweep them clean.
She's crying when I think that. She's crying again.
I have been her, crying. I have been the one to take the tea.
I think of my friend's words,
Remember, someone did it for me.
The doorstep pools with dark souls who want in.
In their inky pockets, they conceal
toy guns with red handles. They want to rob my bank of tissues,
my dugs of milk, my mouth of *there, theres*.
They will always find someone.
They do not need to find me. Her, too. Someone else.
I show her out the back way, lock all the doors,
latch the windows.

Black Ice

A film of molecules separates us from the pavement.

Each car fanning off the side of the road, right and left,
                            is a different disaster.

The wipers are furious, useless.
A smear of headlights shows the curve of guardrails. Hazards blink.

A door opens to the cold and I see the face of a woman turning toward us,
but we don't stop —

The rain becomes skater's ice, most slippery when closest to freezing,
easy to glide across and
                                 the car fishtails right —

        We're suspended in each second, one giving way
                till the next spin is a slow, smooth arc and
                                I grip the vinyl seam of my seat —
We face the headlights of the car that was behind us —

                           *

For a long time after, when I drove and saw, by the side of the road, a certain kind of tree
a tall, singular tree, I'd think hard, *Don't* — though my hands on the wheel wanted it, the
way a Ouija board always spells out the name of someone you know, same as that.

Elevator Pitch

You are in one of the ones built to sway. When there was a fire,
the elevators used to return automatically to the first floor.

Not today. In case of fire, you have been taught: Take the stairs,
always take the stairs, but now they tell you you must not strike out

on your own, you must listen to what you do not want to heed —
Forget the one thing you thought you knew when everything

started to burn. The smoke is fading out the hallway, you hear
scraps of them yelling, their feet knocking on the floor. You hear

Get in the elevator. Because you want to live and because
you have been trained to listen, you listen. You are obedient. You go

against instinct. You go in. You let the doors close around you.
You move down, through, and past the emergency.

The doors open. You are clear. You have now,
and time to think about it.

The Question Under the Question

What has to go unsaid, we nonetheless
keep trying to say. Or I do, anyway — I seem to love
a brick wall as much as Ignatz loves to throw
what it's made of — and like the Kat,
I'm Krazy, trying again, stubborn as I am,
trying again to say it, that which is unsaid —

This is the poet's business: to circle back and try
again. No one minds, no one will even notice
if I keep on with my volleys, rushing headlong
at walls I should be scaling with words or with
the cool turn of my body, moving like a pole valuter's,
to make and be the arc that defies the wall.

Who am I kidding?
Even if I wished for one, I don't have a body like that,
I'm happy with my ladystack, my brick house,
my mighty mighty.

I ask him a second time
if he's heard me, knowing he has. I ask
to underscore the void, as all the ladies
in the nail salon turn and raise their eyebrows
at the end of my second question —

They know this man, what he's doing, know
what it is to be ignored, to ask *Do you hear me?*
To ask for replies that never come.

What would it take to merit an answer?
Wait. I know the answer.

This is the poet's business, to ask better questions,
to ask questions in a way that yields new answers,
to ask the question under the question.

So, let me rephrase.

Not *Do you hear me?*
Not even *What is it you want from me?*
Those old rhetoricals, those curses cloaked as questions.

That is not it, at all. What goes unsaid
is also what goes unasked.

In the park at noon, my shadow strides out
long in front of me, sliding
with great ease onto the walk, then the wall,
then down the passageway
beyond it, as if it were only a question
of how to move as well as a shadow.

I wonder how to move this way:
indelible, smooth, with such confidence.

But my body keeps insisting on itself, so I had
better ask a better question. I had better
want something more. I had better try again.

The question I ask myself, the one my body keeps
making as I sleep, as I traverse the city, as I come out
from inside, the question I am transmitting from sleep to
wake and back under again: *Do I matter?* How do we
come to this, our first and last queer query?

Everything seems booby-trapped. Nothing is alive.
What will spring this open? Not
Do you hear me? I know you hear me.

Mad women, women made mad, women in
a rage asking old questions, I know you.
You are me; I am you.

What will spring this open?

Let's take a walk, you and I, let's fan our hands out in
front of us, let's shake them to blow the polish dry.

These nails are red as brick. No — redder.

And if, as we leave that old scene to wither behind us,
I turn and ask you *Is this the right shade?* know
I'm asking, *Shall we go along together?*
Shall we keep going?

Notes

"*Bench* (1999)" is a response to Isamu Noguchi's *Bench* (1966). In 2018, I learned that, when visiting the Noguchi Museum in Long Island City, New York, the public is now permitted to take a seat on Noguchi's sculpture.

"A Tuesday Spot" was written in response to the poems in Jorie Graham's *Overlord*. The poem refers, in part, to the Protection of Women from Domestic Violence Act that was enacted in India in 2006.

"The Light Table" is for the stained glass artist Kelly Putnam.

"*The Flageolet Player on the Cliff*" refers to the 1889 oil painting by Paul Gauguin of the same name, which lives in the Indianapolis Museum of Art.

"After Looking at Bontecou's *Untitled* (1961)" is a response to wall relief by the American sculptor Lee Bontecou (b. 1931). Bontecou was one of the few female sculptors whose work was recognized by critics in the 1960s. After critics panned a 1971 exhibition of her transparent vacuum-formed plastic fish and flora, Bontecou withdrew from the New York art scene and later decamped to a studio in rural Pennsylvania, where she continued to produce new work. In 2004, *Lee Bontecou: A Retrospective*, an exhibition organized by the Hammer Museum in Los Angeles and the Museum of Contemporary Art, Chicago, was shown at MoMA QNS, in Long Island City.

"The Mechanism of Pleasure" owes a debt of gratitude to Anne for sharing the story of her brain surgery with me.

The term "Room Tone" refers to a recording of the natural ambient silence of a location for a sound editor to use as a reference point, or for when silence is required.

The title "Surface Anatomy of the Head and Neck" is a chapter heading in *Gray's Anatomy* that describes the bones, joints, and muscles of these areas.

"*Les jours gigantesques*" or "*The Titanic Days*," was the suggested title given to René Magritte by his friend, the poet Paul Nougé, for his 1928 oil painting that seems to depict a rape. Magritte's original title was "*La peur de l'amour (Fear of love)*."

"Off the Roosie" borrows its structure from Frank O'Hara's "The Day Lady Died".

"Virtue" is a response to the icon of the Ladder of Divine Ascent, which is located in St. Catherine's Monastery, Sinai Peninsula, Egypt.

"The Question Under the Question" refers to *Krazy Kat*, a comic strip by George Herriman, which ran in American newspapers from 1913 to 1944. In the comic, a cat named Krazy loves Ignatz Mouse, who does not return Krazy's sentiment. Ignatz tries to discourage Krazy's affections by throwing bricks at the cat but Krazy is so besotted that she interprets the bricks as missives of love and sometimes declares, post-whomp, "Oh my Ignatzes! Lil dollin'!"

Acknowledgements

Thanks to Patty Paine and Law Alsobrook of Diode Editions for giving this collection a safe home and for making it the lovely object you now hold in your hands. Warm thanks to Zoë Shankle Donald, Diode's marketing maven, for her care and for getting this book into the world. I raise a sweet glass of lemonade to you three.

Gratitude to Kristy Bowen of dancing girl press for publishing my chapbook *The Hasp Tongue* in 2014.

I offer grateful acknowledgement to the editors of the following journals who first published early versions of some of poems included here: *AGNI, The Antioch Review, Arch, Bateau, Blackbird, The Concher, Day One, Fugue, The Lineup, Margie, Minola Review, Newtown Literary, Octopus Magazine, Poetry East, Prairie Schooner, Print Oriented Bastards, Rascal, SouthWord, The Sycamore Review, Two Weeks,* and *Underwater New York.*

"Gauntlet" appeared in the 2017 anthology *Resist Much, Obey Little: Inaugural Poems to the Resistance* (Spuyten Duyvil).

"Fear Not, Mary," was selected by Kevin Prufer as the winner of the 2015 *Fugue* Poetry Prize and was nominated for a 2015 Pushcart Prize.

"The Hasp Tongue," was awarded a 2008 Academy of American Poets Prize.

Aaron Cohick of NewLights Press created a limited edition broadside of "Meat Cove, Cape Breton" in 2010.

The composer Herschel Garfein created the song cycle "Three Rides," using my poems "The Cyclone," "Black Ice," and "The Mechanism of Pleasure." "The Cyclone" first appeared as a part of the 2016–2017 Five Boroughs Music Festival and had its world premiere in February 2017 in performances throughout New York's boroughs, sung by ace soprano Marnie Breckenridge.

For support — financial and otherwise — thanks to the Helen Zell Writers Program at the University of Michigan, Ann Arbor; the Queens Council on the Arts; the Table 4 Writers Foundation; the Center for Book Arts; the Vermont Studio Center; the Haystack Mountain School of Crafts; and the Prague Summer Program. Thank you to my friends and colleagues at NYU Gallatin, an unparalleled place at which to work.

Heartfelt gratitude for the encouragement of my poetry teachers throughout the years: Tori Kornfield, Carol Farthing, William Carpenter, Lorna (is love) Goodison, Thylias Moss, Linda Gregerson, Marie Howe, Geoffrey Nutter, and Grace Shulman.

Sending love and gratitude to my friends for kindness, support, and guidance (an incomplete list, in order of appearance) : Heather Day, H. Jeremy Schneider, Martin and Lesa O'Connell, Chris Dixon, Danny Littman, Troy Jollimore, Robert Plowman, Anne Higgins, Bregtje van Dam, Andrew Rotch, Douglas A. Martin, Chris Smith, Brenda Copeland, Honor Molloy, Andrew Cohen, Tom Hopkins, Nita Noveno, David Salvage, Danielle Lazarin, Jen Michaels, Celeste Ng, Laura Wetherington, Preeta Pamarasan, Anne Stameshkin, T. Hetzel, Susanne Wise, Kelly Sullivan, Jared Harel, Lisa Jarnot, Jessica Nordell, Nandita Ghosh, Leyla Sharafi, Nancy Agabian, David McLoughlin, Regan Sommer McCoy, Stephanie Feldman, Erin Layton, Bobby Abate, Tom and Emily Hopkins, Meera Nair, Abeer Hoque, Malcolm Chang, Frances Levin, Geoffrey Nutter, Sarah Warren, Emily Fragos, Herschel Garfein, Scott Hightower, Dawn Siff, Nicki Pombier Berger, Nicole Miller, Nicole Hartounian, and all the fine women of SSD and NH.

Of late, solidarity with Faisal Mohyuddin, Ricky Ray, Elizabeth Lindsey Rogers, Afshan D'souza-Lodhi, Kaveh Akbar, Maggie Smith, Lynn Melnick, Dustin Pearson, Cat Conway, Aaron Kent, and Leah Umansky — new friends and fine poets, all.

With love and thanks to my mom, Carol Barrett, for her fierce and ferocious self; my always-laughing brother James; and my sister Kelly, who drew the world for me and kept me from harm.

With love and gratitude for my Sam — the brightest star in my firmament.

KC Trommer is the author of the chapbook *The Hasp Tongue* (dancing girl press, 2014) and is founder of the online audio project QUEENSBOUND. She holds an MFA from the University of Michigan, Ann Arbor, where she was awarded an Academy of American Poets Prize. Her poem "Fear Not, Mary" was selected by Kevin Prufer as the winner of the 2015 *Fugue* Poetry Prize. Her work has appeared in *AGNI, The Antioch Review, Blackbird, LitHub, Prairie Schooner, The Sycamore Review, VIDA*, and in the anthologies *Resist Much, Obey Little: Inaugural Poems to the Resistance* (Spuyten Duyvil, 2017) and *Who Will Speak for America?* (Temple University Press, 2018). She is the Assistant Director of Communications at NYU Gallatin and lives in Jackson Heights, Queens, with her son. You can find her at kctrommer.com.